AF226127

UP IN SPACE

WE BUILT A STATION

BY

MARIANNE J. DYSON
"SPACE NANNA"

www.MarianneDyson.com

Cover design and interior
layout by Lindsey Cousins

Houston, Texas

ISBN 978-0-578-30631-5

For my grandkids
with love,

Space Nanna

Space Shuttle Atlantis heads to
the station in May 2000.

Up in space, we built a station.

Parts came from many nations.

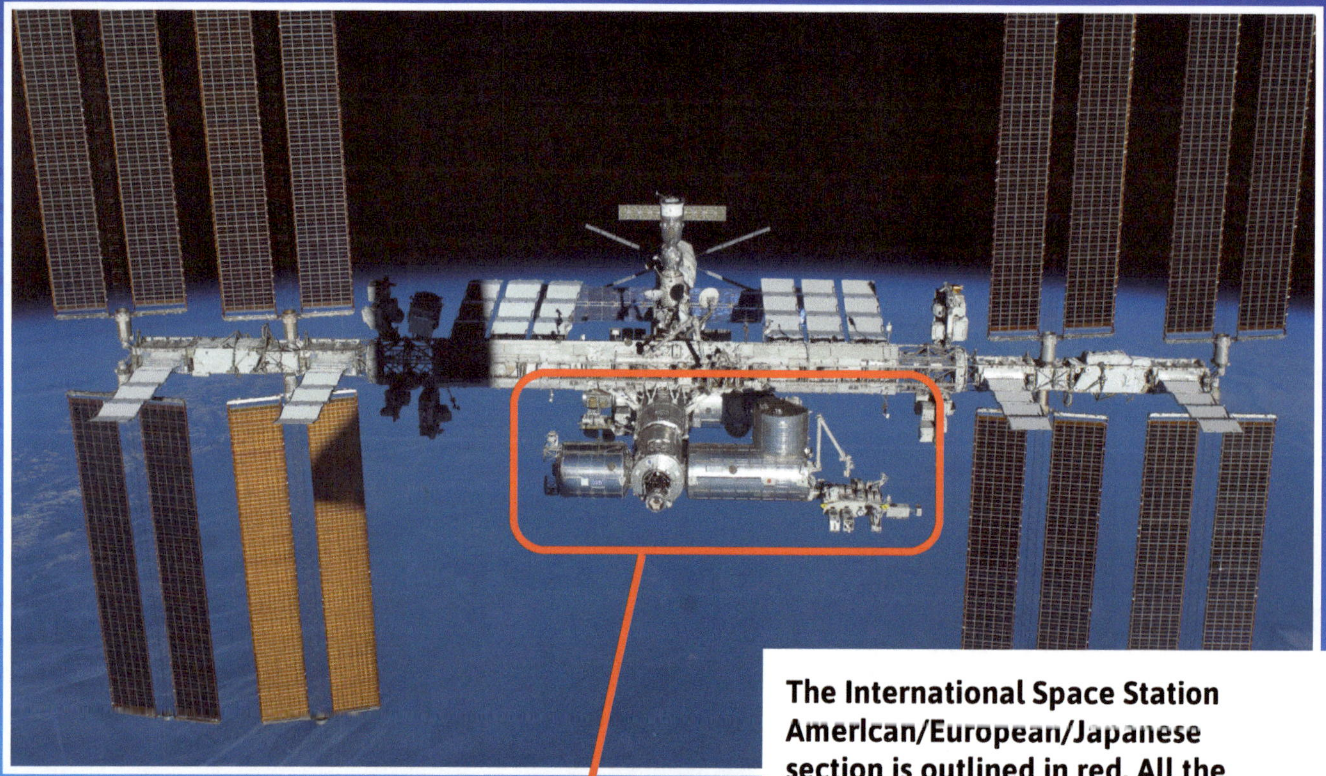

The International Space Station American/European/Japanese section is outlined in red. All the Russian modules are on the opposite (aft) side of the truss.

Some parts of the International Space Station:

1: The truss
2: Canadian robot arm
3: Quest airlock
4: Unity node
5: Tranquility module
6: Logistics module
7: European Columbus module
8: Destiny lab module
9: Harmony node
10: Japanese Kibo lab
11: Japanese exposed facility "porch"
12: Leonardo module

The station from side to side, is a football field wide.

Space shuttles, Atlantis shown at bottom in 2011, brought up American, European, Japanese, and Canadian parts of the station. The solar arrays (112 feet/34 meters long) were folded into boxes and unfurled in space.

A Russian Progress resupply ship is at the top of the image, then the Zvezda ("Star") module and the smaller Zarya ("Sunrise" with folded arrays). A Soyuz crew capsule sticks up from between Zvezda and Zarya.

Rockets carry up the crew, someday, maybe even you!

Rockets boost spaceships to orbit. Shown here is a Dragon capsule atop its Falcon rocket during launch from Florida in 2020.

The SpaceX Crew Dragon Endeavour approaches the station in April 2021. The crew exit the ship through the round hatch in the nose.

All things float because they fall.
In space they have no weight at all.

Japanese Astronaut Koichi Wakata floats in the Kibo Module in 2009.

Moving things in space is fun, a little push, and work is done!

Astronaut Greg Chamitoff and Cosmonaut Sergei Volkov move a rack in the Destiny Lab in 2008.

The crew eat like normal folk, except food and water float!

Astronaut Karen Nyberg enjoys a meal in the Destiny Lab in 2013.

Space toilets are shaped like cans. Waste is sucked away by fans.

The toilet in Zvezda is the can with the white lid. The banded hose has different attachments for men and women. Cosmonauts use the bar on the floor to anchor themselves.

Down below is quite a show.
Volcanoes smoke, hurricanes blow.

Hurricane Felix was seen from space in 2007. The center of a hurricane is called an eye.

Smoke plumes from volcanoes are seen in the Bering Sea near Alaska in 2003.

The sky is black, day and night.
Earth sparkles blue and white.

Earth photographed from the
International Space Station.

City lights shine through the night.
Our planet is a lovely sight!

The Nile River valley was seen at night from the International Space Station in 2021.

Mission Control tracks the crew sends a list of chores to do.

Space Station Mission Control (2015) is in Houston, Texas. The author worked Shuttle flights from this room in 1982.

The Russian Mission Control Center, shown in March 2018, is in Korolev, Russia.

"Hello?" students call from school, HAMs say, "Hello! How are you?"

HAM/Astronaut Sunita Williams talks with students from the Zvezda module in 2007. HAMs are people who use amateur radio.

Hanazono Elementary School students in Akashi-city, Japan called Sunita Williams in 2007.

Solar panels turn and tilt.
The cells form a golden quilt.

Solar array "wings," shown in 2011, turn sunlight into electricity. They look gold from the back.

Radiators look so neat.
White panels get rid of heat.

Radiator panels, shown in 2011, have tubes of ammonia inside that give up heat to space. Panels are white to reflect sunlight. The AMS atop the truss studies dark matter.

Astronauts work many hours, testing flames and growing flowers.

Astronaut Cady Coleman installs a new furnace in the Destiny Lab in 2011. Because hot air doesn't rise in space, flames are round.

Cosmonaut Roman Romanenko poses with a plant grown in the Zvezda Module in 2009.

Sometimes they go out in suits, wearing helmets, gloves, and boots.

Astronaut Ron Garan exits the Quest airlock (see round hatch door above him) in 2011.

Astronaut Alvin Drew waves from the station during a 2011 spacewalk.

Spacewalking is loads of fun, just never look at the sun!

Astronaut Andrew Feustel takes a photo of a materials experiment during a spacewalk in 2011.

Robot arms grapple and fetch, safely catch their Astro "pets."

Spacewalking Astronaut Scott Parazynski "rides" on the Canadian robotic arm to repair a solar array in 2007.

When the day in space is through, astronauts enjoy the view.

Astronaut Sandra Magnus views Earth from the cupola (in the Tranquility Node) in 2011.

Sleeping bags are used for beds. Pillows wrap around their heads.

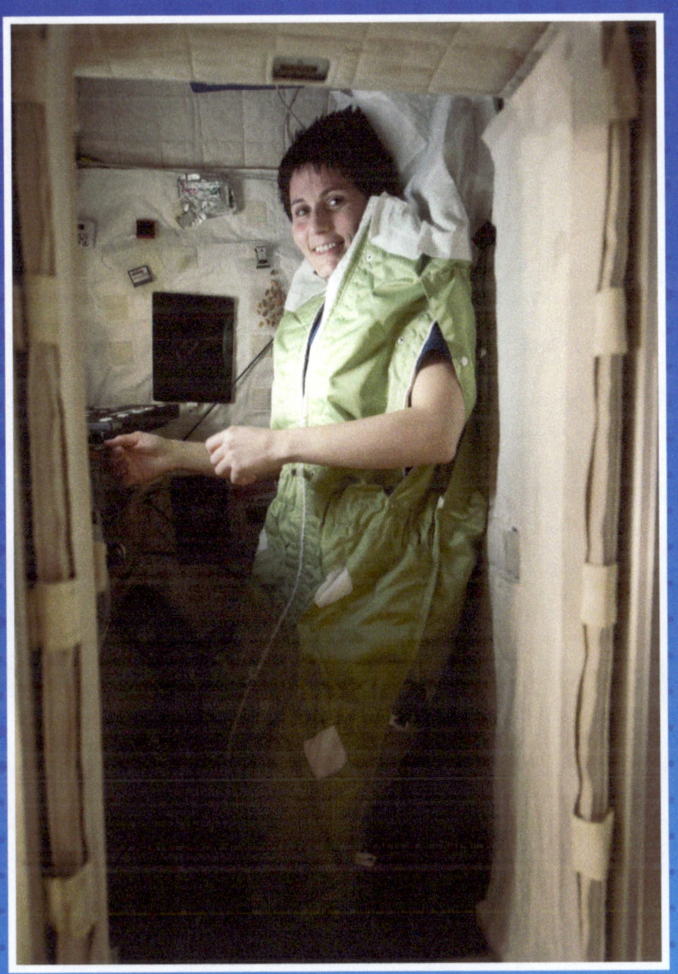

European Astronaut Samantha Cristoforetti has her sleeping bag hooked to the wall in December 2014.

Astronauts Tom Jones and Mark Polansky sack out in Destiny in 2001.

Crew say "Bye!" It's time to go.
They will miss the plasma glow.

Charged particles from the sun strike the atmosphere near the poles and create the aurora or "northern lights" shown here above Canada in 2017.

Parachutes help slow them down. Ships splash! They're safe and sound.

Four parachutes slow SpaceX's Crew Dragon that splashed down in the Atlantic Ocean in 2019.

After splashdown, capsules are loaded onto recovery ships for return to Florida.

Up in space, we built a station. What comes next?

The last Shuttle flight took this "parting shot" of the station in July 2011. The gray dot in the distance is the next human destination: the Moon!

Imagination!

This is what the Earth looks like from the distance of the Moon.

The white dot under the rings is what Earth looks like from the distance of Saturn which is nine times farther from the sun than Earth.

GLOSSARY

ASTRONAUT – a person who flies into space. Called cosmonauts in Russia.

CYGNUS – an unmanned spacecraft built by Northrop Grumman that takes cargo and supplies to space.

DRAGON – a spacecraft built by SpaceX for ferrying humans to space and back.

FREEFALL – weightlessness caused by gravity's pull. Commonly called "zero-g" or microgravity.

GRAVITY – the force that pulls things down.

HAM – amateur radio and its operators.

HELMET – head protection worn by astronauts.

HURRICANE – a big storm with strong winds.

MISSION CONTROL – a team of experts on Earth responsible for spacecraft and crew safety.

MODULE – a can-shaped room for humans in space.

NODE – a room with four hatches to connect station parts.

PARACHUTE – a device that slows an object's fall in air.

PLASMA – charged particles called ions and electrons.

PROGRESS – an unmanned Russian spacecraft that takes cargo and supplies to space.

RADIATOR – a device to release heat into space.

ROCKET – a device that pushes gases out the rear to move forward.

SOLAR PANELS – devices that collect sunlight to make electricity.

SPACEWALK – human travel outside of a spaceship.

SOYUZ – a Russian spacecraft that ferries humans to space.

STATION – a building in space where astronauts work.

VOLCANO – a mountain that releases lava and smoke.

WEIGHT – the amount of heaviness of a person or thing.

European Astronaut Alexander Gerst exercises in Destiny Lab in 2014.

INTERNATIONAL SPACE STATION CONFIGURATION

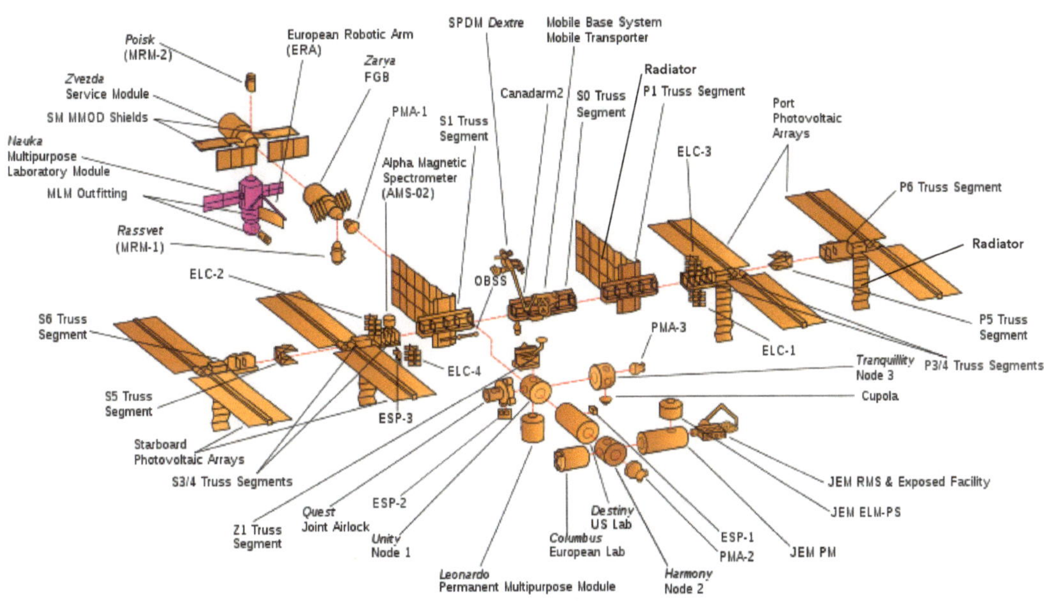

ACRONYMS

AMS – Alpha Magnetic Spectrometer, a physics experiment
ELC – ExPRESS logistics carrier, platforms with power and data
ERA – European robotic arm
ESP – External stowage platforms hold spare parts
FGB – Functional Cargo Block
JEM – Japanese experiment module
MRM – Mini research module (Rassvet means "First Light")
PMA – Permanent mating adapter, a docking port
P1, P3/4, P5 and **P6** – port (right) side truss segments
RMS – remote manipulator system, a robotic arm
S0, S3/4, S5, S6 – starboard (left) side truss segments
SM MMOD – Service Module micrometeoroid and orbital debris shield
SPDM – special purpose dexterous manipulator, a robotic arm

Looking out the window at Dragon in 2021.

FREE FALLING ACTIVITIES

QUESTION 1: WHY DOESN'T THE SPACE STATION FALL TO THE GROUND?

SCIENCE INVESTIGATION

1. Tie a small stuffed toy or rubber spaceship on a string.
2. Toss it straight up while holding the string.
3. Observe that it falls back down.
4. Spin it around your head.
5. Observe that it only stays up when it's going fast.

DISCUSSION

The station doesn't fall to Earth because it goes super-fast: 17,500 miles per hour (28,000 kmph) which is 5 miles (8 km) per second. To come home from space, a spaceship must slow down. The ship's engines and then Earth's air slow it down.

The International Space Station in July 2011. Marianne Dyson photo.

QUESTION 2: WHY DO THINGS FLOAT IN SPACE?

SCIENCE INVESTIGATION

1. Find two containers just alike.
2. Put coins in one. Leave the other empty.
3. Drop the two containers from the same height.
4. Observe containers falling side by side.
5. See them hit the ground at the same time.

DISCUSSION

Gravity pulls light and heavy things down at the same speed. Things falling next to each other only seem to be floating. Everything inside the space station is falling. This is called freefall.

Astronaut Leeland Melvin enjoys a floating meal onboard a Shuttle in 2009.

QUESTION 3: WHY DON'T HEAVY THINGS FALL FASTER?

SCIENCE INVESTIGATION
1. Drop two sheets of paper from the same height.
2. Observe they fall at the same speed and hit the ground together.
3. Crunch one sheet and leave the other alone.
4. Drop them from the same height again.
5. Observe the crunched one hits the ground first.

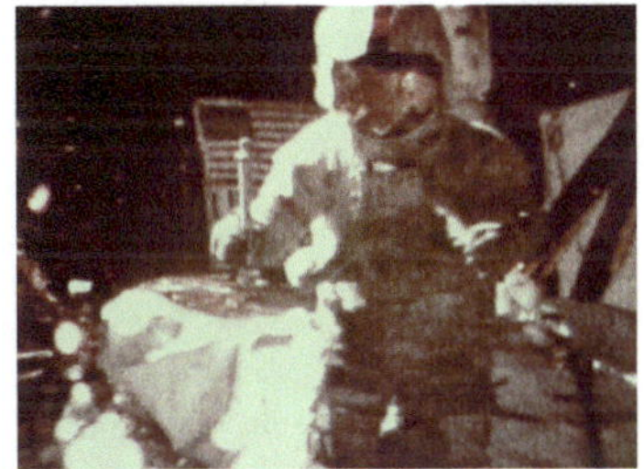

DISCUSSION
The reason shape matters is because on Earth objects fall through an "ocean" of air. This is how parachutes slow down spacecraft. Parachutes won't work on the airless Moon. On the Moon, the crunched and flat papers hit the ground at the same time. Apollo 15 Commander Dave Scott (see photo) dropped a feather and hammer to demonstrate this! Watch the video: https://moon.nasa.gov/resources/331/the-apollo-15-hammer-feather-drop/.

RESOURCES

Amateur Radio on the ISS (ARISS) talk to astronauts.
https://www.ariss.org/upcoming-educational-contacts.html
Space Station official website
https://www.nasa.gov/mission_pages/station/main/index.html
NASA TV: watch launches/crew interviews/spacewalks
https://www.nasa.gov/multimedia/nasatv/index.html
Spot The Station when overhead
https://spotthestation.nasa.gov/sightings/index.cfm
Author Marianne Dyson's website
https://www.MarianneDyson.com

The station viewed from the Russian end looking up in 2011.

PHOTO CREDITS

1-NASA photo iss065e049854. 2-NASA photo STS-099-s-022. 3-NASA photo STS-88-s99_03771. 4-NASA photo s134e010592, taken during STS-134 in 2011. 4b-NASA photo S-134e010585, taken during STS-134 in 2011. 5-NASA photo iss027e03663, taken during STS-135 in 2011. 6-NASA photo NHQ202005300127, 2019. 6b-NASA photo by Astronaut Michael Hopkins, 24 April 2021. 7-NASA photo s020e007312, 2009. 8-NASA photo 017e014091, 2008. 9-NASA photo iss036e025543, 2013. 10-NASA photo iss007e11796, 2003. 11-NASA photo iss015e25044, 2003. 11b-NASA photo iss015e16896, 2007. 12-NASA photo. 13-NASA photo, 2021. 14-NASA photo jsc2015076004 by Bill Stafford, 2015. 14b-NASA photo NHQ201803230003 by Joel Kowsky, 2018. 15b-NASA Image: ISS014E18307, 2007. 15b- Image courtesy of Satoshi Yasuda, 7M3TJZ, 2007. 16-NASA photo s134e011413, 2011. 17-NASA photo iss028e016140, taken during STS-135, 2011. 18- NASA photo ISS026-E-014925, 2011. 18b-NASA photo ISS021-E-012522, 2009. 19-NASA photo iss028e016253, taken during STS-135, 2011. 19b- NASA photo iss026e030929, taken during STS-133 in 2011. 20-NASA photo s134e007597, taken during STS-134, 2011. 21-NASA photo iss16e008932, taken during STS-120 in 2007. 22- NASA photo iss028e017074, taken during STS-135 in 2011. 23-NASA photo iss042e023422, 2014. 23b-NASA photo sts098-355-001, 2001. 24-NASA photo iss053e023965, 2017. 25-NASA photo KSC-20190308-PH_CSH01_0169, 2019. 25b-NASA photo KSC-20190308-PH_SPX01_0001, 2019. 26-NASA photo s135e011914, taken during STS-135, 2011. 27-NASA photo as17-152-23274, taken during Apollo 17 in 1972. 27b-NASA/JPL-Caltech/Space Science Institute photo PIA17171, 2013. 28-NASA photo iss040e006700, 2014. 29-NASA art as of STS-134, 2011. 29b-NASA photo iss065e002465, 2021. 30-Marianne Dyson photo, 2021. NASA photo s135e011814. 30c-Marianne Dyson photo, 2021. 30d-NASA photo 2009. 31-Marianne Dyson photo, 2021. 31b-NASA photo as15_hfd_1, a still from Apollo 15 movie, August 2, 1971. 31c-Marianne Dyson, 2021. 30d-NASA photo s133e011051F. Back cover courtesy Marianne Dyson in Harmony mockup at JSC in 2011.

INDEX

American, 3, 4, 5

Astronaut, 3 (Ross, Newman), 7 (Wakata), 8 (Chamitoff, Volkov), 9 (Nyberg), 15 (Williams), 18 (Coleman, Romanenko), 19 (Garan, Drew), 20, (Feustel), 21 (Parazynski), 22 (Magnus), 23 (Cristoforetti, Jones, Polansky), 28 (Gerst), 30 (Melvin), 31 (Apollo)

Canada/Canadian, 4, 5, 21, 24

Columbus Lab, 4, 29

Destiny Lab, 4, 8, 9, 18, 23, 28, 29

Dragon capsule, 6, 25, 27

Europe/European, 4, 5, 23, 28, 29

Earth, 12, 27, 29

Japan/Japanese, 4, 5, 7, 15, 29

Kibo Lab, 4, 7, 29

Mission Control, 14, 28

Quest Airlock, 4, 19, 29

Robot arm, 4, 21, 29

Russia/Russian, 3, 4, 5, 14, 28, 29, 31

Shuttle, 2, 5, 26, 31

Solar arrays, 1, 5, 16, 21, 28, 29

SpaceX, 6, 25

Spacewalk, 19, 20, 21

Station, 1-6, 12, 13, 19, 26, 28-31

Toilet, 10

Tranquility Node, 4, 22, 29

Unity Node, 3, 4, 29

Zarya, 3-5, 29

Zvezda, 5, 10, 15, 18, 29